T0047100

Life is Not Useful

Critical South

The publication of this series is supported by the International Consortium of Critical Theory Programs funded by the Andrew W. Mellon Foundation.

Series editors: Natalia Brizuela, Victoria Collis-Buthelezi, and Leticia Sabsay

Life is Not Useful

Ailton Krenak

Edited by Rita Carelli

Translated by Jamille Pinheiro Dias and
Alex Brostoff

polity

First published in Portuguese as *A vida não é útil* © 2020, Ailton Krenak
Published in Brazil by Companhia das Letras, São Paulo International Rights
Management: Susanna Lea Associates

This English edition © Polity Press, 2023

2

Polity Press
65 Bridge Street
Cambridge CB2 1UR, UK

Polity Press
111 River Street
Hoboken, NJ 07030, USA

All rights reserved. Except for the quotation of short passages for the purpose of criticism
and review, no part of this publication may be reproduced, stored in a retrieval system
or transmitted, in any form or by any means, electronic, mechanical, photocopying,
recording or otherwise, without the prior permission of the publisher.

ISBN-13: 978-1-5095-5404-1- hardback
ISBN-13: 978-1-5095-5405-8- paperback

A catalogue record for this book is available from the British Library.

Typeset in 12.5 on 17 pt Sabon
by Fakenham Prepress Solutions, Fakenham, Norfolk NR21 8NL
Printed and bound in Great Britain by TJ Books Ltd, Padstow, Cornwall

The publisher has used its best endeavours to ensure that the URLs for external websites
referred to in this book are correct and active at the time of going to press. However, the
publisher has no responsibility for the websites and can make no guarantee that a site will
remain live or that the content is or will remain appropriate.

Every effort has been made to trace all copyright holders, but if any have been overlooked
the publisher will be pleased to include any necessary credits in any subsequent reprint or
edition.

For further information on Polity, visit our website:
politybooks.com

Contents

About the Author

Ailton Krenak was born in 1953 in the Doce River valley region, a territory of the Krenak people and a place whose ecology has been severely impacted by mining. An activist in the socio-environmental movement and in defense of Indigenous rights, he organized the Aliança dos Povos da Floresta (Alliance of Forest Peoples), which unites riverine and Indigenous communities in the Amazon. He is one of the most prominent leaders of the movement that emerged from the Indigenous Awakening in the 1970s in Brazil, and he also contributed to the creation of the Union of Indigenous Nations (UNI). He has done extensive educational and environmental work as a journalist and in video and television programs. His struggles in the 1970s and 1980s were decisive for the inclusion of the chapter on Indigenous rights in the 1988 Brazilian

Constitution, which guaranteed Indigenous rights to ancestral homelands and culture, at least on paper. He is the co-author of the UNESCO proposal that created the Serra do Espinhaço Biosphere Reserve in 2005 and is a member of its managing committee. He was awarded the Order of Cultural Merit of the Presidency of the Republic in 2008, he received an honorary doctorate from the Federal University of Juiz de Fora in Minas Gerais in 2016, and in 2022 he was a recipient of the Prince Claus Impact Award. He is also the author of *Ideas to Postpone the End of the World* (House of Anansi Press, 2020).

About this Book

"You Can't Eat Money" is based on a live-streamed conversation between Ailton Krenak and Leandro Demori for *The Intercept Brasil* on April 8, 2020; a lecture Krenak gave at the event Plante Rio, at Fundição Progresso in Rio de Janeiro, November 2017; and an interview with Amanda Massuela and Bruno Weis called "O tradutor do pensamento mágico," *Cult*, November 4, 2019.

"Dreams to Postpone the End of the World" is based on a live-streamed conversation between Ailton Krenak and Sidarta Ribeiro at the Festival Na Janela, by Companhia das Letras, on May 24, 2020, and the above-mentioned interview with Amanda Massuela and Bruno Weis, "O tradutor do pensamento mágico."

"The Thing-Making Machine" is based on a live-streamed conversation between Ailton Krenak and

Marcelo Gleiser at the Conversa Selvagem, on April 17, 2020; an interview with Fernanda Santana called "'Vida sustentável é vaidade pessoal,' diz Ailton Krenak," *Correio*, January 25, 2020; a live-streamed conversation between Emicida and Ailton Krenak for the GNT channel during Environment Week on June 6, 2020; and a live-stream with Jornalistas Livres on June 9, 2020.

"Tomorrow is Not for Sale" is drawn from three interviews with Ailton Krenak, carried out in April 2020: Bertha Maakaroun's "O modo de funcionamento da humanidade entrou em crise," *Estado de Minas*, April 3, 2020; William Helal Filho's "Voltar ao normal seria como se converter ao negacionismo e aceitar que a Terra é plana," *O Globo*, April 6, 2020; and Christiana Martins's "Não sou um pregador do apocalipse. Contra essa pandemia é preciso ter cuidado e depois coragem," *Expresso*, Lisbon, April 7, 2020. This chapter was published as an e-book by Companhia das Letras in April 2020.

"Life is Not Useful" is based on the conversation "Como adiar o fim do mundo," *O Lugar*, March 18, 2020; a live-stream with Jornalistas Livres on June 9 2020; and the above-mentioned interview with Fernanda Santana, "'Vida sustentável é vaidade pessoal,' diz Ailton Krenak."

Acknowledgments

I am especially grateful to Rita Carelli, who was fundamental to making this book happen, and to Izabel Stewart, for supporting my work and research.

Introduction

Natalia Brizuela

The cosmic sense of life

This phrase condenses one of the many currents in which Ailton Krenak's work has been immersed, deeply, since he was a child in the 1950s, living with his family, and in the public sphere since the 1970s. His interventions, collected in this and numerous other books, essays, and recorded lectures and conversations, remind readers and audiences that the Earth is a living organism, and that humans are but one minuscule element of it. Ailton[1] also reminds us humans that we must awaken from the

[1] Following Brazilian conventions, I will refer to the author by his first name, Ailton. This is how he is known throughout Brazil. The name "Krenak" also refers to the Krenak people, and not only to Ailton, rather than functioning as a family name as it would in the Anglosphere. It is standard practice in Brazil to refer to public figures using only their first name: e.g. Caetano (Veloso), Gal (Costa), Lula (da Silva).

comatose senselessness we have been submerged in since the beginning of the modern colonial project, where order, progress, development, consumerism, and capitalism have taken over our entire existence, leaving us only very partially alive, and in fact almost dead. To awaken from the coma of modernity is, for Ailton, to awaken to the possibility of becoming once more connected to the cosmic sense of life. Through the modern Western project, we have butchered the Earth, "torn it apart," laid it to waste, and with it ourselves. Regaining a cosmic sense of life is remembering that "[l]ife moves through everything" – rocks, mountains, rivers, plants, animals, insects, ancestors – and that it is "crossing the planet's living organism on an immaterial scale." Life is not about what we are able to plan and organize on a calendar, it is not about working enough to be able to rest, it is not about becoming a fulfilled individual with a certified education and a large salary. "Life is transcendence" (p. 14). And because it is transcendence, it cannot be made "useful" within the utilitarian logic of the colonial habitation of the planet. Life, as Ailton states in a 1989 interview, is "assuring the preservation of the universe of relations."[2] Life, for him, is sustaining

---

[2] Ailton Krenak, "Receber sonhos," in *Ailton Krenak* (Rio de Janeiro: Azougue, 2015), p. 93. Originally published as an interview in in *Tendências e Debates*, July 1, 1989.

the connective tissue between visible and invisible beings in this cosmos.

This is why Ailton's questioning of what constitutes humanity is central to this book, from the first phrase of the first essay, "You Can't Eat Money." In this essay as well as the others in this book, based on interviews and conversations that took place primarily during the first months of the COVID-19 pandemic, Ailton emphatically points out that the pandemic affects all so-called "human" lives and that the time is ripe for us all to reflect on and undo the exclusivity and distinctions that have characterized the concept of humanity throughout Western modernity, whereby some humans are part of the "caste" and others are considered "sub-humans" (Indigenous, Black people): "Perhaps the very idea of humanity, this totality we have learned to call humanity, will dissolve with the events that we are currently experiencing" (p. 4). The idea of humanity, as Ailton insists throughout the book, is only an "illusion" disguising the accumulation of power and money by some. Ailton offers, in these and numerous other essays and lectures from the last thirty years, a harsh critique of the forms of division, separation, and rupture – between humans and "sub-humans," between humans and non-humans, between humans and so-called "nature," between so-called "humanity" and the Earth – that constitute the DNA of progress, modernity, and capitalism. Humanity has tried to destroy the cosmic sense of life, but many, particularly those labeled "sub-human," have been actively keeping the cosmic sense alive against all odds given the ongoing genocidal attacks they have suffered on their life forms and practices since the dawn of the colonial project. The development of the "club of humanity" (p. 1) throughout the long modern project is figured by Ailton as the severance of our entanglement with the Earth and with life.

This impoverished human is also incapable of practicing a form of dreaming that sustains "the networks and connections that we have been a part of since ancient times" (p. 15), as Ailton argues in the book's second essay, "Dreams to Postpone the End of the World." This "institution" of dreaming is what holds the relation of all cosmic life in balance. Ailton is calling on humans to awaken from the coma of modernity and embrace a practice of dreaming where the Earth connects with us. He is offering an invitation to leave the paranoias of modernity, the neurosis of individualism, and listen to and feel the presence of all that is around us. Dreaming is an institution and a practice that one learns from elders, that one shares intimately, that offers spacetime for marveling and sensorial sharing. For Ailton, humanity is neither a formless mass of sameness nor a sum of individuals, each striving and in competition to secure their own small plot of property. Humanity is not separate from the Earth, he insists. The Earth is humanity. An awakened humanity is a humanity that dreams and, in dreaming, preserves the "cosmic connections" (p. 19) that constitute the meaning of life and that are made present in daily waking life through dreaming. It is in dreams that the wisdom of the ancestors and the relations with all the entities that belong to the Earth in its material and immaterial dimensions are woven together and actualized. There can be no cosmic sense of life without the practice of dreaming. And it is in dreaming that the narrow, modern definition of humanity can be set aside in favor of an expansive inclusion of all earthly beings. The institution of dreams, sustained by Indigenous people, can help save us from the cancerous capitalism that has "metastasized," "infiltrating life" (p. 22), and can renew in us the ability to live otherwise, as was done in the beginning, as told and practiced by Indigenous people.

For Ailton, postponing the end of the world means having an understanding of time that is not linked to the utilitarian logic of economic power, gain, and efficiency. "*Um tempo além desse*": Ailton says that a time beyond the present time will need to dream other dreams because dreams are what allow us to be welcomed by the world, to be in it, and to inhabit it. Dreams are "a fantastic, promising source of hope" (p. 24). Dreaming is key for the making of new, different worlds based on dignity and respect.

Awakening

Ailton rose to prominence in Brazil among both Indigenous and non-Indigenous people in the 1970s. Born in 1953, he was a child of the first generation of Krenak people to live "in captivity," since the Krenak ancestral land in the region of the Rio Doce was occupied by the Brazilian state in 1922, and the Krenak people, like numerous other Indigenous people throughout Brazil in the early 20th century, were forced to live on a reservation. By 1968, Ailton's extended family, among many others, were again forced into exile, having to leave the reservation as part of the then newly exiled generation of Indigenous people. He arrived in São Paulo in 1975, attended Western schools, studied graphic arts, and quickly became involved in the then emergent awakening of Indigenous people that mobilized towards the creation of the Union of Indigenous Nations (UNI/União de Nações Indígenas) in 1983.

A set of laws enacted in the early 20th century had forced Indigenous people into tutelage with the Brazilian state. This tutelage – aimed at exterminating Indigenous lives through the joint projects of "civilizing," "integrating," and land occupation – was first exercised by Brazil's Indian Protection Services (SPI/Serviço de Proteção aos Índios) between 1928 and 1967. In the aftermath of international media scandals revealing corruption and charges of human rights abuses leveled against the SPI — some of which dated back to the 1950s — the National Indian Foundation (FUNAI/Fundação Nacional do Índio) took over from the SPI in 1968. These governmental agencies were key to the state's project of development and frontier expansion.

In the mid-1970s, news began circulating that the military government was going to issue an "emancipation decree" dissolving the decades of tutelage. The government's maneuver was meant to disguise its genocidal plot behind a smokescreen of humanitarianism, when in fact the decree would allow it to articulate a cruel and violent lie: that the Indigenous people had finally become completely assimilated, and therefore there were no longer any Indigenous people left for the Brazilian state to "protect" through tutelage. This perverse strategy of political annihilation would allow the government to take over the reservations and other ancestral lands. And thus began the devastation of the Amazonian Basin region, among others, through mega-projects like the Transamazonian Highway (BR-230) and the Perimetral Norte highway (BR-210).

The decree was one of numerous fronts in a ferocious developmentalist strategy undertaken by the military government. Indigenous inhabitants of non-urban-dwelling regions throughout Latin America suffered a sustained genocidal wave in the 1970s, resulting from the state's renewed territorial expansion into the last remaining untapped lands as capitalism entered its neoliberal phase. In the early years of neoliberal rule, private developers, through agreements with anti-democratic governments, saw the lands inhabited by Indigenous peoples as the last frontier for their predatory schemes. The 1978 Treaty for Amazonian Cooperation is a case in point. Signed by the governments of Brazil, Venezuela, Colombia, Ecuador, Peru, Bolivia, Guyana, and Suriname, the pact promised to both "develop and protect the Amazon basin, one of the last remaining great open spaces of the world." The treaty's articles centered on the promotion of "harmonious development" of the Amazonian territory, for the "preservation of the environment and the conservation and rational utilization of the natural resources of these territories."[3]

The "awakening of Indians," as Ailton described the 1970s in a 2013 interview, occurred as Indigenous

---

[3] *New York Times*, July 4, 1978. For further reading, see Peter Calvert, "Amazon Cooperation Treaty, 1978," *Encyclopedia of US–Latin American Relations*, vol. 1 (2012): 12–13.

peoples rose up to resist occupation and disappearance.[4] In 1974, Indigenous leaders from across the country began meeting, first in the National Assemblies of Indigenous chiefs, and by 1979 in a series of meetings that in 1983 led to the founding of the regionally structured Union of Indigenous Nations. Ailton took on the role of coordinating publications for the UNI's Southern region, in São Paulo, and from 1985 onwards, he was the national coordinator of publications and communications. This is the context for his own path to political leadership. But his own awakening, as he recounts it in "Dreams to Postpone the End of the World," came from a dream shared with him in the late 1970s by a shaman who told him of the Earth's devastation by the white people's projects. Ailton was given that dream, which he then shared with Indigenous people as he began traveling throughout Brazil and building the movement. He realized that "there was something in Indigenous peoples' perspective, in our way of seeing and thinking, that could crack open a window of understanding in the environment that is the world of knowledge" (pp. 16–17). Two years after the UNI was established in 1983, and as he took charge of communications

---

[4] See Ailton Krenak, "Eu e minhas circunstâncias," in *Ailton Krenak*, p. 243. Interview originally published in *Nau* (December 2013).

and publications for the movement, he co-founded the Indigenous Culture Center, and within that organization launched the first ever Indigenous-produced radio program in Brazil, *Programa de Índio*, which aired between 1985 and 1990. He produced over 200 programs about the traditions and cultural practices of Indigenous peoples inside and outside Brazil, which were aired through a station belonging to the University of São Paulo and distributed as cassette tapes to numerous Indigenous villages throughout the country.[5]

"My work in the UNI is my life," Ailton stated in a 1984 interview, "because my life will only gain meaning if I am able to redeem an identity. What is that? It is affirming the existence and the right to existence of all Indians in Brazil."[6] Alongside Marçal Guarani, Angelo Pankararé, Ângelo Kretã and Domingos Terena, Paulo Bororo, Paulo Tikuna, Lino Miranha and Álvaro Tukano, among others, Ailton fought for *the right to existence*, against misinformation about assimilation. This is one reason why the category of life is so central in his thinking. Against death, he advocates life. Against disappearance, appearance. And this is what his

[5] You can access a number of the radio programs here: http://ikore.com.br/programa-de-indio/.
[6] See Ailton Krenak, "A União das Nações Indígenas," in *Ailton Krenak*, p. 22. Originally published in *Lua Nova* (June 1984).

participation in the UNI did, along with that of others: make Indigenous life visible, audible, and undeniably vibrant, creative, and alive.

In accounts of Ailton's life, 1987 is usually mentioned as the time when he became "famous," and he definitely did because of the televised recording of his speech before the Brazilian Congress that year, which went viral immediately. The Brazilian Constitution was being rewritten, and part of UNI's organizing during the 1980s involved drafting a set of demands that the hundreds of Indigenous groups, very much alive, wanted written into the new legal document to ensure the possibility of a future. They were not so much interested in being equal citizens of a predatory state as they were in strategically inscribing their existence within the state's apparatuses and legal infrastructure.

In his address to the Brazilian Congress as UNI's spokesperson, delivered on September 4, 1987, Ailton, dressed in a white suit, slowly painted his face with black dye from the jenipapo tree in front of the members of the Constituent Assembly. As he painted his face, he said, "Indigenous people have a way of thinking, a way of living,"[7] one that never puts any animal or human at risk.

[7] See   https://www.youtube.com/watch?v=TYICwl6HAKQ for Ailton Krenak's 1987 speech, where he says in Portuguese: "o povo indígena tem um jeito de pensar, tem um jeito de viver."

They were "respectfully" asking to have that way of thinking and living protected. His dramatic performance and its immediate viral reception are considered to have been instrumental in pushing the Brazilian Constituent Assembly to grant almost all of UNI's demands, which were included in the 1988 Constitution. Their four main demands were met: recognition of historical rights of Indigenous peoples; the demarcation of Indigenous lands; the guarantee that the Indigenous collectives would be the sole users of the natural resources in the demarcated territories; and the Brazilian state's compliance with the future-oriented projects (*projetos de futuro*) of Indigenous populations. Instead of being "emancipated" and therefore eradicated, Indigenous people delivered a demand that Ailton voiced and performed: the demand to be recognized as citizens and as Indigenous people.

Ailton's own awakening was spurred in the 1970s by the predatory practices of the insatiable capitalist machine that continues to devastate the Earth and life. That devastation inevitably required – and continues to require – the destruction of Indigenous lives. This is why it is important to pay attention to when and how Ailton intervenes, and does so in a brilliantly conceptual, tongue-in-cheek manner, to shake us all up and awaken us from the nightmarish political and environmental catastrophes we participate in and unconsciously support. For example, "Tomorrow is Not for Sale," included as an essay in this book, was first distributed freely as an e-booklet in April 2020, during the early months of the COVID-19 pandemic. In the essay, he urges us to take the tragic context to reorganize our lives so as to permanently remove ourselves from the clock time of the market.

Listening with the collective-constellation

All the texts in this book, like almost all the texts Ailton has published, originated as conversations, lectures, and debates that were then transcribed and edited. In fact, the section in this and other books by him titled "About this Book" reveals what we could call his method. In numerous instances, texts are elaborated by others, in consultation with him, based not on one but on several live conversations, interviews, and presentations that are then edited into a single text. This weaving of ideas is supported by their dwelling in memory and the transformation through their encounters with new environments, situations, and people. Ideas are developed in and through conversation, in a brilliant radiance of conceptual thinking produced in movement. Conversations and interviews are dialogic encounters through which alliances can be established. We could think of all of Ailton's public presentations, interviews, conversations, and texts as ways of building alliances through a politics of reciprocity, articulating and performing a new relationality between Indigenous and non-Indigenous people. The orality at the origin of Ailton's text is the form chosen for the radical notion of relationality that he offers to us as non-Indigenous people. Dialogue, exchange, relation, and reciprocity are key notions in his thought, and in the oral form, they become the structure of a praxis – one based on listening.

It would be easy to mistake this for an example of Indigenous people's "oral cultures" as these are described in a host of deeply racist historical misrepresentations. But Yasnaya Aguilar, the Mixé linguist, writer, and activist, reminds us, along with numerous Indigenous scholars, activists, and artists, that Indigenous people do not have "oral traditions," but rather "mnemonic traditions."[8] The idea of "oral cultures" or "oral traditions" has been used to distance Indigenous people from so-called "writing cultures," as a way of separating those who encounter the world through reason from those who inhabit it in a "natural" and hence pre-civilized manner. Western modernity, with its

[8] See Yasnaya Aguilar Gil, "(Is There) an indigenous Literature?", trans. Gloria Chacón, *Diálogos* 19.1 (Spring 2016), p. 158.

countless institutions and homogenizing temporal framework, always sees the oral as preceding the written, as falling somewhere behind in the chronology of development. But as Ailton and many other Indigenous people explain, the practice and activation of memories – through dreaming, singing, dancing, storytelling, and various other activities – are ways of belonging to and sustaining the cosmic sense of life.

Without listening, there can be no exchange, no reciprocity, no conversation, no encounter, no relation. "Either you hear the voices of all the other beings that inhabit the planet alongside you, or you wage war against life on earth" (p. 38), Ailton claims in the last sentence of "The Thing-Making Machine." Listening to all the other beings that live alongside the human means building the connective tissue, the invisible vibratory link and connection that sustains a vast plurality of entities and life forms. Listening means being alive, staying alive, and keeping the ecosystems to which one belongs alive as well. Listening is caring. Not listening brings war: that is, a type of destructive encounter, a form of non-co-existence. We listen with our entire bodies, not just our ears. Bodies are, for Ailton, the most necessary, precious, and precise pieces of equipment needed to alter the destructive actions and insatiable greed of the capitalist machine. Our bodies are part of and an extension of the Earth. If we allow them to become sensing instruments for dreaming and conversation, the cosmic sense of life would not be so threatened.

The conversation is among humans, all humans, but also, as Ailton points out in "The Thing-Making Machine" and "Dreams to Postpone the End of the World," with animals, plants, rivers, mountains, and all ancestors. Indigenous memories of the origin of life tell of a time when humans were fish, trees, rivers. This is why the Krenak people, for example, "have bonds with the river, the rocks, the plants, and other beings" (p. 20). In these texts and numerous other presentations and interviews, Ailton urges us to think about the ways in which we are part of constellations – "We walk as constellations" (p. 19) – rather than of communities. As constellations constituted of visible and invisible beings, we would inevitably have to stop destroying the Earth, because we would recognize everything on it as our relatives and not as raw materials with which to make things we can consume and commercialize.

Constellation, as Ailton uses the word, is what causes us to engage in making worlds, all the time. It also signals what he calls, in a beautiful interview from 2018, the "collective subject."[9] By this, he

---

[9] Ailton Krenak, "A potência do sujeito coletivo," https://revistaperiferias.org/materia/a-potencia-do-sujeito-coletivo -parte-i/.

means an organizational model based on common access: to water, food, sociability, ancestors, territoriality. The collective-constellation travels and moves through the world of "life" together with the entire cosmic order. For Ailton, the collective subject lives in an enlarged world, one that does not isolate, distinguish, delimit, and exclude through forms of bordering. The enlarged world is a world made in part by the collective subject, where the real power of creativity is experienced. Ailton uses the Portuguese word *potência*, which is not synonymous with the Western notion of hegemonic power. It should be understood as an alternative form of power, one that is grounded in a never-ending expansion of the here and now. *Potência* is linked to bodies, specific singular bodies, human and non-human in relation to each other, rooted. The potential universes of creation and invention, of enlarged and expansive worlds, are part and parcel of the *potência* of the subject as collective, as always in flux and in the making. Faced with numerous attempts to destroy the collective's *potência*, the collective has re-organized, regrouped, expanded, regained its *potência*, and fought back. This happened in the 1970s during the genocidal attacks against Indigenous peoples and communities. As Indigenous peoples approached the brink of forced disappearance, they returned in the form of a collective subject, in the case of Brazil through completely new alliances among Indigenous peoples from hundreds of different regions, with countless cosmologies. For Ailton, the Indigenous organizations and mobilizations in Brazil that resulted in, for example, the inclusion of Indigenous rights in the 1988 Constitution, or the demarcation of the Yanomami Territory in 1992, were reactions against the "obliteration of our existence, against the negation of our historical rights and of our possibilities for inventing other ways of being." The *potência* to resist the end of the world will be collective and should be led by the cosmic sense of life practiced by Indigenous peoples.

This book was originally published in Brazil in late August 2020, and Ailton's previous book, *Ideas to Postpone the End of the World*, in 2019. As this book goes to press, his newest, *Ancestral Future*, has been published in Brazil in December 2022. The historical context of the two books is different, and yet sadly very similar, to the specific historical context of Ailton's awakening in the 1970s. Once again, the Brazilian state is attempting to eradicate the Indigenous population by denying their existence. Since the early 2000s, a new wave of attacks against Indigenous lives have been underway in the country. In 2021, the Bolsonaro administration gave new life to a bill first presented to Congress in 2007 known as PL 490/2007 or, in its most recent revival, the "temporal framework" bill, which wanted to set a cutoff date of 1988 for Indigenous people to have legal rights to claim their territories and to be considered Indigenous. Any groups that had not legalized their lands and their identities as Indigenous before that date would have no claims over ancestral lands. This would in turn facilitate even further deforestation and mining projects, which could be legalized through another bill under discussion since 2020, PL 191/2020. The latter would allow for mining mega-projects in Indigenous lands, thus canceling the gains made in 1987 when Ailton gave his speech to the Constituent Assembly. Then, like now, Ailton addresses us as a way to awaken us into political action. To save ourselves. To create alliances and relations with the Earth. To guide us towards a cosmic sense of life.

You Can't Eat Money

When I speak of humanity, I am not only talking about *Homo sapiens*. I am referring to a vast array of beings that we have always excluded. We hunt whales, we fin sharks, and we kill lions and hang them on walls to show that we are braver than them. I am also talking about the killing of all the other humans who we thought had nothing, and existed for the sole purpose of providing us with clothes, food, and shelter. We are the plague of the planet, a kind of giant amoeba. Throughout history, humans – or rather this exclusive club of humanity, which appears in the Universal Declaration of Human Rights and in institutional protocols – have been devastating everything around them. It is as if they had elected a caste, named it humanity, and judged all those who are outside of it as sub-human. Not only the *caiçaras*,[1] *quilombolas*,[2] and Indigenous peoples, but all forms of life that we deliberately left by the wayside. And that "way" is progress: the notion that we are going somewhere. We assume that there is a horizon, that we are heading to it, and on the way, we drop everything that does not matter, everything that is left, sub-humanity – some of us are part of it.

It is amazing that this virus out there now is only affecting people. It was a fantastic trick by Earth as an organism to pull its teat out of our mouths and say, "Now breathe, I want to see you breathe." This exposes how the kind of life that we have created became artificial, because at some point you will need a mask and a breathing apparatus, but that apparatus also depends on a hydroelectric dam or a nuclear power plant or some kind of power generator. And that generator may also fail, regardless of our ambition or intent. We are being reminded that we are so vulnerable that if air is cut off for a few minutes, we die. It

---

[1] *Translators' note*: *Caiçaras* are traditional populations living alongside the southern Brazilian coast who are descended from Indigenous, Black, and Portuguese ancestors. Their livelihood is primarily based on small-scale fishing and agriculture.
[2] *Translators' note*: *Quilombolas* are descendants of fugitive enslaved communities, or (former) maroon communities (*quilombos*), which have maintained cultural and religious traditions throughout the centuries.

doesn't take a complex warfare system to extinguish this so-called humanity: it is extinguished as easily as mosquitoes in a room after repellent is sprayed. We humans are not all-powerful – the Earth declares it.

And if we are not all that great, we should have the experience of being alive beyond the technological apparatuses that we can invent. For example, think about the economy, which is an invisible thing, except for that "$" sign. Perhaps it is a fiction to say that if the economy does not fully function, we die. We could put all the leaders of the Central Bank[3] in a giant safe and let them live there with their economy. You can't eat money. This morning I saw a Native American from the council of elders of the Lakota people talking about the coronavirus pandemic. He is a man in his mid-seventies called Wakya Un Manee, also known as Vernon Foster. (Vernon is a typical American name, because when the settlers arrived in America, besides banning native languages, they also changed people's names.) Quoting an ancestor, he said, "Only when the last tree has been cut down, the last fish been caught, and the last stream poisoned, will we realize we cannot eat money."

---

[3] *Translators' note*: Brazil's Central Bank, or "Banco Central," is the financial institution that formulates and administers monetary and credit policies in the country.

Perhaps the very idea of humanity, this totality that we have learned to call humanity, will dissolve with the events that we are currently experiencing. If that is the case, what will happen to the guys – and there are only a few of them – who keep the world's money? Maybe we can knock them off their feet. Because they need humanity, even if it is an illusion, to terrorize them every morning with the threat that the stock market will drop, that the market is panicked, that the dollar will rise. When all of that becomes meaningless – screw the dollar, to hell with the market! – then there will be no more room for such a concentration of power. Because only in certain environments can such concentration occur. Even pollution: what happens if it spreads out without being contained? The air becomes cleaner. Didn't pollution in cities decrease when we slowed down? I believe that the illusion that there is a caste of humanoids holding the secret to the Holy Grail – gorging themselves on wealth while terrorizing the rest of the world – may eventually implode. Perhaps the most recent sign of that is how those billionaires are building a platform outside of the Earth where they could move and live. I don't know exactly where, maybe Mars. We should say: "Go on, just leave and forget about us!" We should give them a free pass; a free pass to the owners of Tesla, of Amazon. They can leave us their address and we will send them supplies.

It seems like the notion of the concentration of wealth has come to a climax. The entanglement of power and capital has reached such a degree of accumulation that the political and the financial management of the world can no longer be separated. There was a time when there were governments and revolutions. There were plenty of the latter in Latin America: Mexico in the 19th and 20th centuries was a real laboratory for them. This culture of revolutions, in which people take action, overthrow governments, and create other forms of governance, no longer makes sense today. Not in Latin America, nor in Africa, nor on any other continent. This is because governments no longer exist. We are now governed by big corporations. Who is going to overthrow the corporations? It would be like fighting ghosts. Power is now an abstraction concentrated in brands merged into corporations and represented by a few humanoids. I have no doubt that these humanoids, spellbound by the power of money, will also reach a saturation point. We are experiencing a gradual change in the conditions for life on this planet and we will all be brought down to the same level. Both trillionaires and you and I will all face the same fate.

These people who hold all the wealth have the nerve to live in areas where they can be shielded from illnesses, each with their own personal ventilator. What they are unaware of is that the power source for their secret bunkers can also be switched off. No matter what apparatus they are setting up, they could end up like that astronaut in *2001: A Space Odyssey*, who is disconnected from his capsule while taking a spacewalk. So who knows? Maybe this cream of the crop – these guys who have long been used to watching the world die from the towers of their castles – will have to experience as big a risk as anyone else. Some critics may disagree and say that these guys have always had an extraordinary ability to transform crises into an opportunity to increase wealth concentration, but this also has a limit. Even the laws of physics show that nothing can be indefinitely concentrated, which is why some nuclear reactors leak – or explode.

We are addicted to modernity. Most inventions are an attempt by us humans to project ourselves into matter beyond our bodies. This gives us a sense of power, of permanence, the illusion that we will continue to exist. Modernity has these artifices. The idea of photography, for example, which is not so recent: projecting an image beyond that moment in which you are alive is a fantastic thing. And then we get stuck in a kind of senseless looping. This is an incredible drug, much more dangerous than the ones that the system bans out there. We are so doped up by this wicked reality of consumption and entertainment that we become disconnected from the Earth's living organism. With all the evidence – the melting glaciers, the oceans full of garbage, the increasing lists of endangered species – could ripping up the Earth be the only way to show the denialists that it is a living organism? Tearing it into small pieces and showing them: "Look, is it alive?" It is absurdly stupid.

James Lovelock, who developed the Gaia hypothesis, was kicked out of a NASA research program, marginalized by the folks who overestimated Darwin's theory. For them, the notion that the Earth is a living organism was unscientific. Until the late 1990s, any research that approached this organism as an intelligent thing would be written off. Thomas Lovejoy, known as the father of biodiversity studies, as well as a number of researchers working on the Gaia theory, had dispersed. The status of some of these scientists was devalued to the point where there was no one to fund their research anymore. Of course, some of their followers are still active: here in Brazil, for example, we have Antonio Nobre, who has been carrying on with these speculations about the different languages that the Earth's organism uses to communicate with us. However, in the last five or six years, with the escalation of the climate crisis and the planet boiling up, these deniers have begun to refrain from their skeptical perspective, expressing their wish to understand the Gaia theory. I leave this to the unbelievers. Those who already heard the voice of the mountains, the rivers, and the forests do not need a theory about this: every theory is an effort to explain to the hardheads the reality that they cannot see.

Whether in a forest or in a flat, we need to awaken our inner power and stop looking for culprits around us, be they corporations or the government. Because all those things come to an end, and we cannot have an expiration date like theirs. We should not wait for the government, supermarkets, or any of those factories that package everything to send us supplies. Most people not only eat things that seem to be poisoned, like strawberries and tomatoes, but they do not even know what a lot of things that they consume are. If you read the nutritional information of a given product, it is full of words whose meaning you do not understand. Now, how are you going to believe that? They may have processed all sorts of rubbish and are giving it to you to eat. That is why it would be much better if we took care of our little seeds, saw them sprout, looked after them, and then harvested them. Only then will we know where what we eat comes from.

Through agroecology, through permaculture, there are people in different places fighting for this planet to have a chance. These micropolitics are gaining momentum and will take the place of the disillusionment caused by macropolitics.

The agents of micropolitics are people planting vegetable gardens in their backyards, opening up space in the pavement to let sprout whatever may be. They believe it is possible to undo the concrete tomb of metropolises. I think a lot about Gilberto Gil's song "Refazenda," about those lines that say: "Abacateiro/ acataremos teu ato/ nós também somos do mato/ como o pato e o leão" (Avocado tree / We will accept your act / We are also from the woods / Like the duck and the lion). Time has passed, people have concentrated on metropolises and the planet has become a toothpick holder.[4] But now, emerging from within the concrete, comes this utopia of transforming urban cemeteries into life. Agroforestry and permaculture show the people of the forest that there are people in cities making new alliances possible, without setting cities on one side and the countryside on the other.

Someone might say, "But we are not going back to being an agricultural society!" Probably not, in part because what we are doing around the world is not really agriculture. There is this immoral campaign that says "agro is tech, agro is pop, agro

---

[4] *Translators' note*: The metaphor "the planet has become a toothpick holder" gestures at the fragility of urban verticalization, in which skyscrapers are increasingly crammed up alongside one another while people are increasingly crammed inside them.

is everything,"[5] in which they show the whole process of industrialization, not only of food, but also of ore. Everything has become agro. Ore is agro, robbery is agro, stealing from the planet is agro, and everything is pop. Agro is to blame for the calamity that we are facing on the planet today.

Here in my region, Vale[6] is looking like the stock exchange: nervous. Since the world stopped, it has accelerated. Trains pass three to five hundred meters from my house. Only a comatose river separates us from the railroad.[7] And the trains are gigantic: the Earth shakes as they pass. The coming and going doesn't stop, all night, all day. I even kept thinking: are they making the final heist? They're worse than before, their fever has risen. I think a ship, somewhere in the world, called out: "Send everything, hurry up over there!" We need to look at our

[5] *Translators' note*: "Agro is tech, agro is pop, agro is everything" is the slogan of the advertising campaign "Agro, the industry-wealth of Brazil," created by the Brazilian television station Globo in 2016 to promote agribusiness.
[6] *Translators' note*: Krenak is referring to Vale S.A. (formerly known as Companhia Vale do Rio Doce), which is a Brazilian multinational mining corporation. It has been responsible for two massive dam disasters (Mariana in 2015 and Brumadinho in 2019), among myriad other incidents of environmental catastrophe.
[7] *Translators' note*: In this context, "a comatose river" refers to the Doce River in the aftermath of the catastrophic toxic mudflow caused by the Mariana and Brumadinho dam disasters.

inner being, and not keep overestimating the train that passes outside. We have to stop developing and start getting involved.

When everything is going into a tailspin, you have to have someone to call – I call on Carlos Drummond de Andrade. For me, he is one of those colorful parachutes that I mention in *Ideas to Postpone the End of the World*. "O homem; as viagens" ("The Man; the Travels") is a poem about what we are experiencing:

> Restam outros sistemas for a
> do solar a col-
> onizar.
> Ao acabarem todos
> só resta ao homem
> (estará equipado?)
> a dificílima dangerosíssima viagem
> de si a si mesmo:
> pôr o pé no chã
> do seu coração
> experimentar
> colonizer
> civilizer
> humanizer
> o homem
> descobrindo em suas próprias inexploradas
>   entranhas
> a perene, insuspeitada alegria
> de con-viver.

> There are other systems out there
> than the sun to col-

onize.
when everything comes to an end
only man remains
(will he be equipped?)
the most difficult, most dangerous journey,
from himself to himself:
to step on the ground
of his heart
to test out
colonize
civilize
humanize
man
discovering in his own unexplored entrails
the perennial, unsuspected joy
of co-existing.

Drummond is my shield. We'll still discover fantastic secrets from him in the future, like the insight that man landing on the moon coincided with a rocket being sent into space.[8]

At the time, NASA represented one of the West's shared projects of speculating about space, but recently it has partnered with public–private billionaires who have the crazy idea of creating a biosphere, a copy of the Earth. That copy will be as mediocre as they are. If a part of us thinks we can colonize another planet, it means we still

[8] *Translators' note*: Here, Krenak is referring to an earlier moment in the poem in which the speaker notes this particular coincidence.

haven't learned anything from our experience here on Earth. I wonder how many Earths these people need to consume before they understand that they are on the wrong path. I also don't know how we are going to decipher this "BHP–Samarco–Vale"[9] enigma, the complex that involves the extraction, processing, and shipping of our mountains to other corners of the planet. The ones that Milton Nascimento cries for in his songs when he sees them being devoured. At some point Drummond's poems and Milton's songs meet.

In the 1990s, I went to other places; then I came back to Minas to spend more time here. I needed to re-establish a relationship with this place where mountains are made of wind: they exist to be consumed. I kept thinking about the tragic fate of the territory that bears this name, Minas Gerais. Diamantina too, with miners going there to extract diamonds, precious gems – this obsession with drilling holes in the ground. The place where I am is called the Iron Quadrangle. It's in really bad taste to give names like these to a place. What does it mean? That we're screwed. Two dams, one in Mariana and the other in Brumadinho, spewed iron over us. The long process of developing these technologies,

[9] *Translators' note*: Samarco is a private mining company. It is jointly owned by Vale and Broken Hill Proprietary (BHP). They are among the largest mining corporations in the world.

which fills us with pride, has also filled the rivers with poison. I talked about butchering the Earth, but it won't be necessary: the machinery that these guys shove into the mountains, what happened in the Rio Doce basin – that river seared through by the mud from mining – is such an invasive probing of the Earth that it has already torn it apart.

Here, on the other side of the river, there is a mountain that guards our village. Today it dawned covered with clouds; it rained and now clouds are flying over its summit. Looking at the mountain is an instant relief from all pain. Life moves through everything, through rock, the ozone layer, glaciers. Life goes from the oceans to solid ground; it crosses from north to south like a breeze in all directions. Life is this crossing of the planet's living organism on an immaterial scale. Instead of thinking about the Earth's organism breathing, which is very difficult, let's think about life passing through mountains, caves, rivers, forests. We have trivialized life to the extent that people don't even know what it is and think it is just a word. Just like there are the words "wind," "fire," "water," people think there may be the word "life," but there isn't. Life is transcendence; it's beyond the dictionary; it doesn't have a definition.

Dreams to Postpone the
End of the World

When I ask if we are really a humanity, I propose that we reflect on what actually shapes humanity. This is an opportunity for us to question whether our notion of humanity entails the networks and connections that we have been part of since ancient times. It gives us the chance to ask ourselves if the contribution that those folks in the caves gave to the collective unconscious – an ocean that never depletes – is related to our nerve endings, our endings here, in this distant era. If we reverse the binoculars, instead of looking at our ancestors as those who were here long ago, we will be perceived by their gaze. Sidarta Ribeiro offers some very interesting insight: the hunting scenes in cave paintings may be not only a record of daily activities but also an account of dreams. We have always been able to see the difference between our waking experiences and the world of dreams, so we can surely bring stories from this other world into our waking consciousness.

The kind of dream I am referring to is an institution. An institution that welcomes dreamers, and where people learn different languages, drawing on various resources to reckon with themselves and their surroundings. A hunter's surroundings, for example, appear in cave drawings dating back 20,000, 30,000 years. Today, the dreams of someone who worries about cataclysms, about the planet's environmental tragedy, may be similar to those dreamt by a Xavante shaman, like the one who called me in the Roncador Mountains in Central Brazil forty years ago. A man called Sibupá lived there, near the Xingu Indigenous territory, in the Pimentel Barbosa Indigenous land. One day, this old man called his adopted nephews – myself among them – and told us:

> I had a dream in which the spirit of the prey was very angry and said I was irresponsible, that I was not taking good care of the animals' spirits, that the *waradzu* [the whites] were preying on everything and that soon there would be no more hunting and people would have nothing left to eat.

In this shaman's vision, which young people were asked to share, the Earth would be laid waste.

It was then that I realized that there was something in Indigenous peoples' perspective, in our way of seeing and thinking, that could crack open a window of understanding in the environment that is the world of knowledge. At that time, I started to visit the forests in the states of Acre, of Rondônia, and everywhere I went the shamans said, "You have to be careful because the world of white people is invading our existence." Invading, they said. At that time, I listened to the elders as a bystander, until I started to have the same premonitory dreams when I saw the roads, the tractors, and the chainsaws coming; the noise of them cutting down the big trees and the rivers revolting. I could hear the rivers speaking, sometimes angry, sometimes outraged. We've ended up becoming a nerve ending of what they call "nature." And the science of that shaman, warning an entire generation that is now fifty, sixty years old that their territory would be devastated and left without game, turned out to be absolutely right. Agribusiness invaded Brazil's savannah hinterlands – the Cerrado – and the Xingu Indigenous territory became a pizza; or, rather, a little pie surrounded by soybeans, with tractors cutting everything down. Since then, I have been experiencing the meaning of dreaming as an institution that prepares people to relate to everyday life.

This institution also affects more domestic spheres. Dreaming is a practice that can be under-stood as a cultural regime in which, early in the morning, people tell each other about the dream they had – not as a public practice, but as an intimate one. You don't talk about your dreams in public, but you share them with the people with whom you have a relationship. This also suggests that dreams are a place for conveying affection. I mean affection in the broad sense. I am not only talking about your mother and your siblings, but also about how dreams affect the sensory world; how the act of sharing your dreams with others creates connections between the dream world and the dawn of a new day; and how sharing them with your companions transforms that into intangible matter right away. When dreams are finished being told, those who listen can already pick up their tools and go about their day's activities: the fisherman can go fishing, the hunter can go hunting, and those who have nothing to do can rest. There is no veil separating dreams from everyday life, and they emerge with wonderful clarity.

There are many kinds of dreams. If someone invites me to take a trip, I wait and see if I dream about it. If I don't dream about a trip or an invitation to go somewhere, it means I'm not leaving the place I'm in. I never know in advance what I'm going to do next. This kind of guidance can be thought of as magic, but in fact, it is our way of living. As long as we hold on to it, we will continue to be who we are. This experience of having a collective consciousness is what guides my choices. It is a way to preserve our integrity, our cosmic connections. We may walk around here on Earth, but we walk in other places as well. Most of our Indigenous kin do this. Just look at the work of the Indigenous youth who are publishing, speaking, and interacting with the fields of art and culture. You can see this collective perspective in them. I don't know any individual from any of our communities who has gone out into the world alone. We walk as constellations.

The Krenak are kin to the Xavante, the Krahô, the Kayapó. We are a Jê people.[1] So let's say that we are hunters, not growers. I believe that the cosmovisions and mindsets of hunter-gatherers still persist, even in an adverse situation in which there is nothing left to hunt or gather. In contemporary times, these traditions still have a direct connection with our subjectivity, so hunters dream in one way and farmers in another. There is an ancient story of the Krenak people which describes how the Creator left a humanity here on Earth and went to some other place in the cosmos. One day he remembered us and said, "Oh, I left my creatures there on Earth. I need to see what they've become."

[1] *Translators' note*: The Krenak language is part of the Jê family, belonging to the Macro-Jê linguistic branch.

But as he made this incredible gesture to come here to see us, he thought, "What if they have become something worse than I can conceive? The best thing would be not to have a personal encounter with them. Here's what I'll do: I'll shapeshift into another creature to see my creatures." He then transformed himself into an anteater and went out into the meadow until a group of hunters, armed with cudgels and ropes, approached some bushes, attacked him, caught him, and took him back to the camp with the obvious intention of eating him. Two twin children, who were watching the scene, prevented him from being taken to the fire pit. He then revealed himself to the boys, who covered up his escape before the adults could find out. From the top of a hill, the boys cried out, "Grandfather, what did you think of us, of your creatures?" And God answered, "So-so."

The Krenak notion of the human creature is precarious. Human beings have no certifiable quality; they can go wrong. The notion that humanity is predestined is nonsense. No other animal thinks like that. The Krenak are wary of the idea that there's such a thing as human fate, which is why we have bonds with the river, the rocks, the plants, and other beings with whom we are related. From an existential perspective, it's important to know with whom we can connect, instead of being convinced that we are all that great. It was this viewpoint that made me say that we're not the humanity we think we are. What I'm saying is more or less as follows: if we believe that humans are the ones calling the shots on this wonderful organism that is the Earth, we end up making the serious mistake of thinking that humans are exceptionally special. Well, if this were so, we would not be discussing the indifference of some people to the death and destruction of that which sustains life on the planet. Destroying the forest, the rivers, destroying landscapes, as well as ignoring that there are people dying, shows that humanity has no criteria for quality at all, that this is nothing but a historical construction unconfirmed by reality.

This is clearly demonstrated by the 20th century and all its wars. A kind of armistice had to be arranged, because we armed ourselves to such an extent that we were capable of destroying the planet – several times over. In fact, if our technical skills have led us this far, then we have already given sufficient proof of how disqualified we are, of how we have been abusing other beings: all of them are offended by our impudence. If we Brazilians are ashamed of what happened in our country, there must be millions of beings in the biosphere looking at our dreadfulness and asking, "What are these humans doing?" We are going through a global tragedy. Even if some human communities think above the waterline,[2] they are just a small sample of this humanity. In the midst of all this, we need to put together some kind of vision to get us out of this swamp.

This thing that the political and economic sciences call capitalism has metastasized, occupying the entire planet and infiltrating life in an uncontrollable way. After this pandemic, if we want to reconceive the world without changing this framework, we will have to face the clear fact that what we are experiencing is a crisis, in the sense of a mistake. But if we realize that we're going through a transformation, we will have to admit that our collective dream of a world and the presence of humanity in the biosphere will have to be different. We can inhabit this planet, but we will have to do so otherwise. If we don't take steps in this direction, it would be as if someone wanted to get to the highest peak of the Himalayas but wanted to take along their house, their fridge, their dog, their parrot, their bicycle. They'll never arrive with heavy luggage like that.

---

[2] *Translators' note*: Krenak invented the expression "thinking above the waterline" ("pensar além da linha d'água"). In conversation with the translators, he described how it designates "a poetics of life that has not yet succumbed to the current tsunami of ignorance and negationism," or "the immense multitude of people below the waterline whose senses have dulled, and who are alienated from civic responsibility."

We will have to radically reconceive of ourselves to be here. And we yearn for this newness. It may surprise us. It will have the meaning of Caetano Veloso's poetry in the song "Um índio" ("An Indian"):[3] it will surprise us by being obvious. Suddenly it will become clear that we need to change the equipment we use. And – surprise! – the equipment we need in order to be in the biosphere is our body, precisely.

Some people have an understanding that our bodies are related to everything living, that the cycles of the Earth are also the cycles of our bodies. We observe the earth, the sky, and feel that we are not detached from other beings. My people, as well as other kin, have this tradition of lifting up the sky. When it gets too close to the Earth, there is a type of humanity which, because of their cultural experiences, feels that pressure. It is seasonal; here in the tropics, sky and Earth get closer at the beginning of spring. When that happens, we must dance and sing to lift up the sky, so that changes in the health of the Earth and all beings take place in this process. When we do this ritual, which is called

[3] *Translators' note*: In "Um índio," Veloso sings about an Indigenous person who will reveal things that are already present and accessible to us. Krenak's point is that it is obvious that we need to reconceive ourselves, leave our "heavy luggage" aside and "change our equipment" if we want to continue sharing life on Earth.

taru andé, what gives us power is our communion with the web of life.

Lifting the sky means broadening everyone's horizons, not just those of humans. It is a memory, a cultural inheritance from the time when our ancestors were so in tune with the rhythm of nature that they only had to work a few hours a day to provide for everything that they needed to live. The rest of the time, you could sing, dance, and dream: everyday life was an extension of dreaming. And the relationships, the contracts woven in the dream world were still meaningful after you woke up. When we think about the possibility of a time beyond this one, we dream about a world where we humans will have to be reconceived in order to move around. We will have to give shape to other bodies, other affections, and dream other dreams in order to be welcomed by this world and be able to inhabit it. If we look at things this way, then what we are experiencing today will be not only a crisis, but also a fantastic, promising source of hope.

The Thing-Making Machine

The various Indigenous narratives about the origin of life and our transformation here on Earth are memories of when we were, for example, fish. Because there are people who were fish, there are people who were trees before imagining themselves as human. We were all something else before becoming people – this message runs through the narratives of our Ainu relatives, who live in northern Japan and Russia, and the Guarani, the Yanomami, relatives who live in Canada and the United States. Who knows, maybe even those very ancient people, the Mesopotamians, had stories of this nature? Amerindians and all peoples who have ancestral memory carry recollections of what they were before they were shaped as humans.

When Indigenous peoples refer to a people as "a nation that stands on its feet," they are making an analogy with trees and forests, thinking of forests as entities, vast intelligent organisms. In those moments, the genes we share with trees speak to us and we can feel the grandeur of the planet's forests. This feeling again mobilizes people to protect the forests, an idea which has already become trivialized. There are associations that are created to protect the forest, to create nature reserves, and right here my neighbor, Sebastião Salgado, has a place called Instituto Terra. This is a small sample of the devastated region of the mid-Doce River, which has been tended in order to show people that it is possible to restore the forest. Each of us – not the economy, not the whole system – can act positively in harmony in this chaos.

In the past forty years, the fight to curb deforestation has even turned into a World Bank or UN project, and yet everything has proved ineffective. We couldn't stop deforestation on the planet. The only forests planted with great efficacy and volume capacity are the short-lived ones, which in six to eight years are cut down to turn into cellulose. What I'm trying to say is that my individual choice to stop cutting down the forest cannot negate the fact that the planet's forests are being devastated. My decision not to use automobiles and fossil fuels, not to consume anything that increases global warming, does not change the fact that we are melting. And when the planet becomes another

1.5 degrees Celsius warmer, many species will die before us. That polar bear roaming the Arctic is already looking like a lost dog. He's starving, his complexion has changed, he's sick; it hurts to see that bear. I don't think it was a publicity stunt to use his image to show how predatory we are in the Arctic.

During the pandemic, it was impressive how we responded to the call to stay at home and socially distance ourselves. With the exception of a few eccentrics, everyone agreed to do it. Now, if we are all simultaneously able to heed such an order to stay at home, why wouldn't we be able to hear the order to stop preying on the planet? To stop destroying rivers and forests? This is a transcendent value.

Many people claim that what distinguishes us from other beings is language; the fact that we speak, make judgments, and create social relationships. Now, if humanity's key characteristic is to distinguish itself from the rest of life on Earth, then this idea brings us closer to works of science fiction that suggest that the humans who are inhabiting Earth are not from here. In the midst of this time hanging in suspension, full of surprises, a friend I have been communicating with for a long time told me: "You know, Ailton, these people here on Earth probably came from other constellations. They were androids and had a dark past; that's why they carry this machinery disease." It made me think that the Greeks, at some point, began to perceive the Earth as a mechanism, and I found that terrifying. But who knows, maybe not all humans are from here, or, rather, humanity is made up of many pieces? We are nations, tribes, constellations of people spread across the Earth with different memories of existence.

Friends who work with the history of philosophy and technology have told me that humans' sense of belonging to the totality of life shifted when they discovered that they could appropriate a technique: to act on land, on water, on wind, on fire, even on storms, which were previously interpreted as the effect of a supernatural power. In the traditions I share, supernatural powers do not exist. All power is natural, and we participate in it. Shamans participate in it. In their varying cosmogonies, the shamans leave and go to other places in the cosmos. There is a terran transit ("terrans" instead of "earthlings," because that way, if they are not from here, they are still included) on Earth and beyond.[4] In his book *The*

[4] *Translators' note:* here, Krenak echoes Bruno Latour's notion of "terrien" and Déborah Danowski and Eduardo Viveiros de Castro's "terrano." In the English translation of Danowski and Viveiros de Castro's *The Ends of the World*, the translator explains how "in the Gifford Lectures, Latour renders the French *Terriens* as 'Earthlings' or, more frequently, as 'Earthbound people,' playing on the adjective's multiple connotations: the people who are *destined*

Falling Sky, Davi Kopenawa tells us about this transit in the Yanomami cosmovision. There's a guy who is the Sun's nephew and is related to the Yanomami. I thought the idea of someone related to him being joined with a star was wonderful – not in a symbolic sense, but in a real one. For someone who can negotiate something of interest for his house with the Sun, because he is his nephew, a godson, a brother-in-law. This kinship between the Earth's inhabitants and beings or organisms that are outside has been especially interesting to me in this time of conflicting ideas. Many suggestions of worlds are appearing, always accompanied by the idea that these worlds are in conflict with each other. I don't understand this moment we're living in as a limit case. I think what we're going through is a sort of refocusing in which we have the opportunity to decide whether or not we want to push our own self-extinction button, but the rest of the Earth will continue to exist.

I can't imagine us apart from nature. We can distinguish ourselves from nature in our minds, but not as an organism. The possibility of surviving

---

to the Earth, who are *tied* to the Earth, who are *under the spell of* the Earth . . . We have chosen the name 'Terrans' to designate this demos, which, as shall be seen, Latour opposes to 'Humans' and/or 'Moderns,' taken as synonymous ways of referring to the same people, namely, 'us' " (*The Ends of the World*, trans. Rodrigo Nunes, Cambridge: Polity, 2017, p. xii).

with bodies on Mars or on any other planet will depend on such complex devices that will make it easier to stay here with masks and ventilators (and look, we haven't even realized that). These incredible technologies that we're using today, which connect us, give us a strong dose of illusion. They are like trophies that science and knowledge have given us and that we use to justify the trace we are leaving on Earth.

The planet is telling us: "You went crazy. You forgot who you are and now you're lost, believing you've achieved something with your toys." Well, the truth is that all that technology gave us was toys. The most advanced one even gets people to outer space; this is also the most expensive. It's a toy that only thirty or forty guys can play with. And, clearly, there are some billionaires who want to play, which makes me think that this imaginary humanity, beyond its tremendous spiritual child-ishness, cannot criticize its own history. A history that, most of the time, is a disgrace. What is there to be celebrated about the fact that we can talk to 3,000 or 4,000 people on a little device which is the product of a civilization that is consuming the Earth to make toys? The thing is that the Earth is a much larger organism than we are; it's much wiser and more powerful, and *we* are its most useless toy. The Earth can shut us down by taking our air away. It doesn't even need to make a noise.

Fossil fuels, which the world depends on today, should have been given up by the 1990s – all the reports at the time said so. Since then, the number of things made from oil has increased alarmingly. We have known about the destruction of the ozone layer since the turn of the 1980s. How is it possible that you've been warned that you're drilling into the roof of the sky and the most you can do is get a new refrigerator? Today, if we ask someone who is twenty or thirty years old to question all this, that guy might say: "But now that it's my turn, you're here to tell me that the party's over?" There's a desire for this condition of consuming life to last indefinitely, without ever needing to turn the thing-making machine off.

The capitalist system has such powers of co-optation that whatever crap it advertises immediately becomes a fad. We are all addicted to newness: a new car, a new machine, new clothing, something new. People have said: "Ah, but we can make an electric car; without gasoline, it won't cause pollution." But it will be so expensive, so fancy, that it will become a new object of desire. We know that we need to renounce the things that are ruining our life on the planet. The problem is that people want to renounce such things for other newer and nicer things. Would they have the guts to simply install an electric motor in that car that already exists? Why manufacture a million more cars? These people must not know about Havana, because there are cars there from the 1950s, from 1947, from 1936 – I don't know from when, but everyone makes do with them. Or will we just give up when we can no longer get the next toy?

On the other hand, science has gotten so advanced that people think they don't have to die anymore. Science and medicine have extended human life with a thousand devices, but they've left out people's choice to live within the cycle of life and death that nature allows. And in this way, the possibility of human life proliferating on the planet has expanded, occupying it in an uncontrollable way. We continue to use technological and scientific artifices to endorse the fantasy that everyone will have food, everyone will have a refrigerator, everyone will have a hospital bed, and everyone will die later. Today, people want to be born in hospitals and then live sheltered from the possibility of dying. This is a falsification of life. If we want to change our eating habits, we could also think about changing our practices around being born and dying. I'm not immortal and I don't want to immortalize myself. Science and technology think that humanity can not only get away with impacting the planet without consequences, but will also be the last surviving species and the only one to take flight when everything goes down the drain.

So, it could be that those last gatecrashers who arrived from another galaxy for the party on Earth are so harmful that they end everyone's party and still blast off into space. That's why I say that we are much worse than this virus that is being demonized as the plague that has come to eat the world. We are the plague that has come to devour the world. Some people are aware of this and cry out desperately. Chico Mendes, for example, died crying out. The other day a public authority here in Brazil asked, "Who was this guy?" In other words, what Chico did doesn't even mean anything to a fellow citizen who occupies a position of privilege and leadership in our society and who had an obligation to know who the man was. Many people have already forgotten who Mahatma Gandhi was. Many don't even know who Martin Luther King was anymore. That's why I think the proverb "one swallow doesn't make a summer" conveys an interesting message.

Just this morning, I remembered something Gandhi said when an English journalist asked him about the struggles to liberate India from the British Empire: "There are too many people on the planet. Do you think the Earth can meet everybody's demand?" He was always questioned about modern Western thought, and replied: "The Earth has enough for all of our needs. But if you want a house on the beach, an apartment in the city, and a Mercedes-Benz, there isn't enough for everyone." I have always admired Gandhi's integrity and the simplicity he preached. There is a book that was published in Brazil in 2019 by David Wallace-Wells, *The Uninhabitable Earth*, which shows that all of the world's attempts to regulate the consumption, production, and distribution of goods are unsustainable. The bill doesn't add up.

Capitalism wants to sell us the idea that we can reproduce life, that you can even reproduce nature. We end up with everything and then make something else. We end up with fresh water and then earn a lot of money by desalinating the sea, and if that's not enough for everyone, we eliminate a part of humanity and leave only the consumers – a sort of Big Brother ruling the world according to the whims of capitalism. Some people suggest that those who know how to live in the world are the rich, and that poverty is responsible for the destruction of the environment. This statement, in addition to being racist and classist, is murderous. Because someone in the rich person's position who is saying that the poor – who make up 80% of the world's population – are destroying the planet may also end up suggesting that the poor don't need to live anymore. The truth is that we don't need anything that this system can provide for us, but the system also takes away everything we have. When a councilman appears in your community saying that he is going to clean it up, you have to be suspicious, because when they say that, in general it is us who they want to make disappear. Colonialism is ingrained in the minds of the councilmen, the mayor, the governor, all of the people who have the privilege of pushing a button, opening a gate. These guys keep acting in the service of invasion.

Milton Santos, who stood out in the public debates on globalization, said that it had implications for everyday life, culture, the organization of the work world, and even the idea of wealth and poverty. He called into question the very paradigm of capitalism: he knew that another world could not be a reproduction of this one. But for many people, in Western epistemology, the idea of another world is just another fixed-up capitalist world: you take this world, send it to the garage, change the chassis, the windshield, fix the axle, and start running it again. A rotten old world dressed up like new. I'm definitely not willing to help pay this bill. For me, it's not worth fixing.

In *Spheres of Insurrection*, Suely Rolnik says that capitalism underwent such a significant transformation that it became necrocapitalism: that is, capitalism doesn't need the materiality of things anymore, but can turn everything into a financial fantasy and pretend that the world is functioning and active, even when everything is going down the tubes. It's a dystopia: instead of imagining worlds, we consume them. After we eat the Earth, we're going to eat the Moon, Mars, and the other planets. The same difficulty that many people have in understanding that the Earth is a living entity, I have in understanding that capitalism is an entity that we can deal with. It's not an entity, but a phenomenon that affects the lives and mental state of people all over the planet – I don't see how to be in dialogue with that.

What I'm interested in is the journey we're taking here, in search of a sort of balance between our movement on Earth and the constant creation of the world. For the creation of the world was not an event like the Big Bang, but it's something that happens every moment, here and now. The very geophysical event of the planet's existence in the cosmos is an active event. Everything that we think already existed is happening now. If people can grasp that, they will be able to feel that this world, which we believe exists from different perspectives, continues transforming. "On this day the world was created" is not recorded on a timeline.

I believe that our notion of time, our way of counting it and seeing it as an arrow – always going somewhere – is the basis of our deception, the origin of our detachment from life. Our Tukano, Desana, and Baniwa relatives tell stories of a time before time. The Mayans and other Amerindians also have these narratives, which are plural. They are stories from before this world existed and that even allude to its duration. Familiarity with these narratives greatly expands our sense of being; it takes away our fear and prejudice against other beings. Other beings are here with us, and the re-creation of the world is always a possible event, at all times.

The experience of being in flux in this way clearly gives us the feeling that the pandemic is not the greatest calamity on the planet. If we get stuck with the notion that the way the world works cannot change or be changed, the conception of commodities, control and domination, of course we're going to be terrified, but try getting out of that car, try having a cosmic relationship with the world. Many people must think that only shamans – or people who have already reached some form of transcendence – can have this experience, but what they call science is constantly confirming the relationship between the Earth and the solar system, between galaxies. Let us summon the experience of harmoniously inhabiting the cosmos: it is possible to experience this in our daily lives without surrendering to all the terrorism of modernity.

Many people from different cultural origins have an understanding that we and the Earth are the same entity, that we breathe and dream with it. Some attribute the same vulnerabilities to this organism as our own bodies have. They say this organism has a fever. It makes sense: aren't we made up of two-thirds water and then the solid stuff, our bones, muscles, skeleton? We are microcosms of the organism Earth. We just need to remember that.

Until the beginning of the 20th century, the world of work and production took place with tools and means that did not have the same power to exhaust the Earth's resources as they do today. Today, only a few of these nearly human types of humanity are left scattered around the planet. As the world is entirely unequal, some people – people who are not engaged in planetary consumption – have been left outside of the civilizational knot. They have not become consumers in the sense of a clientele. Eventually, they consume something from the industrial world, but they don't depend on it to survive. There are still islands on the planet that remember what they are doing here. They are protected by this memory of other world perspectives. These people are the cure for the planet's fever, and I believe they can positively infect us with a different perception of life. Either you hear the voices of all the other beings that inhabit the planet alongside you, or you wage war against life on Earth.

Tomorrow is Not for Sale

I stopped traveling around the world. I canceled appointments. I am with my family in the Krenak village, in the mid-Doce River. For almost a month, our Indigenous territory has been in isolation. Those who were not here have returned, and we really know the risk of receiving outsiders. We know the danger of being in contact with asymptomatic people. We are all here and so far we have not had any cases of COVID.

The truth is that we have been living trapped and as refugees in our own territory on a 4,000-hectare reserve (which would be much larger if justice were served) for a long time, and this involuntary confinement has made us more resilient. How can I explain the meaning of my isolation to a person who has been in lockdown for a month in an apartment in a big metropolis? I'm sorry to say this, but today I already planted corn, I already planted a tree ...

It has been some time since we in the Krenak village have been mourning our Doce River. I didn't anticipate that the world would make us grieve this way too. Everybody is standing still. When engineers told me that they were going to use technology to restore the Doce River, they asked my opinion. I answered: "My suggestion is very difficult to put into practice. Because we would have to stop all human activities that affect the river's body, a hundred kilometers on the left and right banks, until it comes back to life." Then one of them said to me, "But that's impossible." The world cannot stop. And yet the world stopped.

Today, we are living this experience of social isolation – as lockdown is called – in which people all have to retreat for a while. If for a while it was us, Indigenous peoples, who were threatened with the breakdown or extinction of the meaning of our lives, now we are all facing the fact that it is becoming almost unbearable for the Earth to provide what we demand from it. We are witnessing the tragedy of people dying in different places on the planet to the point that in Italy, truckloads of bodies are being transported to incinerators.

This pain might help people to answer the question of whether we are really a humanity. We have become used to this notion, which has been naturalized, but nobody pays attention to the true meaning of what it is to be human anymore. It's as if there were several children playing, and because of how we fantasize about a certain image of childhood, they continued playing indefinitely. But what happens is that we become adults. We are devastating the planet, digging a gigantic chasm of inequalities between peoples and societies. There is thus a sub-humanity that lives in extreme poverty with no chance of getting out of it – and this has also been naturalized.

The president of the Republic said the other day that Brazilians jump into the sewage and never catch any diseases.[1] What we see this man do is an exercise in necropolitics, a deadly decision. It is a sick mentality that is taking over the world. And we now have this virus, an organism from the planet, responding to this sick thinking of humans with an attack on the unsustainable way of life that we have adopted by free choice – this fantastic freedom that everybody loves to claim, but which comes at a cost no one thought to ask about.

This virus is discriminating against humanity. Just look around. Bitter melons keep growing right next door. Nature moves on. The virus does not kill birds, bears, any other beings, only humans. The

---

[1] *Translators note*: Krenak is referring to Jair Messias Bolsonaro, who was Brazil's 38th president.

ones who are panicking are the human peoples and their artificial world, since their way of functioning has gone into crisis.

What's happening is terrible, but society needs to understand that we are not the salt of the earth. We have to let go of anthropocentrism. There is so much life beyond us. Biodiversity can do well without us. From an early age, we learn that there are lists of endangered species. While these lists grow, humans proliferate, destroying forests, rivers, and animals. We are worse than COVID-19. This heavy package called humanity is becoming totally disconnected from the organism that is the Earth, living in a civilizational abstraction that suppresses diversity and denies the plurality of life forms, existence and habits.

The only populations that rest assured that they need to hold on to this Earth are those that have been somewhat forgotten on the edges of the planet, on the banks of rivers, on the shores of oceans, in Africa, Asia, or Latin America. They are a sub-humanity: *caiçaras*, Indians, *quilombolas*, aboriginals. There is a humanity that is part of a select club that does not accept new members, and a more rustic and organic layer, a sub-humanity, that is holding on to the Earth. I don't feel part of that select humanity. I feel excluded from it.

For a long time we have been lulled into the story that we are *the* humanity, and we alienated ourselves from this organism of which we are a part, the Earth. We were led to think that the Earth is one thing and that we are another. My perception is that there isn't anything that isn't nature. Everything is nature. The cosmos is nature. Everything I can think of is nature.

We, humanity, are going to live in artificial environments produced by big corporations who own the money. Now this organism, the virus, seems to have had enough of us. It seems to want to disconnect itself from us just like humanity wanted to disconnect itself from nature. It wants to "shut us down" by taking away our oxygen. When COVID-19 attacks the lungs, patients need a ventilator, a device to supply oxygen, otherwise they die. How many of those machines will we have to make for the over 7 billion people on the planet?

Our mother, the Earth, gives us free oxygen, puts us to sleep, wakes us up in the morning with the rising sun, lets the birds sing, moves the currents and the breezes, and creates this wonderful world for us to share. And what do we do with it? What we are experiencing may be the work of a loving mother who decided to shut her child up, at least for a moment. Not because she doesn't like him, but because she wants to teach him something. "Hush, child." That is what the Earth is saying to humanity. And it's wonderful that it isn't giving an order. She is simply saying, "Hush." This is also the meaning of retreating from social life for a while.

If only I could magically get us out of this confinement, a magic that could make everyone feel the rain falling. It is time to tell our children stories, to explain to them that they shouldn't be afraid. I'm not a preacher of the apocalypse. What I try to do is to share the message of another possible world. To fight this virus, we must first be careful and then we must be brave.

We realize some people are against shutting down businesses, arguing that, inevitably, "some people are going to die." This kind of approach affects people who love the elderly, people who are grandparents, parents, children, siblings. It is a foolish claim. It makes no sense for anyone in good conscience to make a public statement saying "some people are going to die." It is a trivialization of life, but it is also a trivialization of the power of words. Someone who says such a thing is issuing a death sentence, both to the elderly and to their children, grandchildren, and all the people who love each other. Imagine if I could be at peace thinking that my mother or father was disposable. They are the reason I am alive. If they are disposable, so am I.

Stupid governments think that the economy can't stop. But economic activities depend on us, since they were invented by humans. If humans are at risk, any human activity ceases to matter. Saying that the economy is more important than us is like saying that a ship matters more than its crew. People who say this sort of thing have a thirst for power and think that life is a meritocracy. We cannot pay the price we are paying and keep making the same mistakes.

In his fundamental work *Discipline and Punish*, Michel Foucault states that this market society in which we live considers human beings useful only when they are producing. As capitalism advanced, instruments that enable us to live and cause us to die were created. When someone stops producing, they become an expenditure. You either produce the conditions to survive or you produce the conditions that cause your death. What we know as social security, which exists in every country with a market economy, comes at a cost. There are governments that think it would be great if all the people who represent expenses were to die. In other words, you can let those who are in the risk groups die. This is not a slip of the tongue; people who say that are not crazy. They are lucid. They know what they're talking about.

My communion with what we call "nature" is an experience long scoffed at by city folk. Rather than see any value in it, they poke fun at it by saying things like "He talks to trees, he's a tree-hugger; he talks to rivers, he contemplates the mountains," as if this were some kind of alienation. But that's my experience of life. If that is alienation, I'm alienated. I haven't scheduled anything for "later" in a long time. We have to stop being presumptuous. We don't know if we'll be alive tomorrow. We must stop putting tomorrow up for sale.

I think of those verses by Brazilian poet Carlos Drummond de Andrade: "Stop / Life has stopped / or was it the car?" The stop we are experiencing is for real. The rhythm of life today is not the same as it was last week, nor is it that of New Year's Eve, or last summer, or January or February. The world is hanging in suspension. And I don't know if we will come out of this experience the same way as we went in. It is like a hook pulling us into consciousness, a jolt to make us face what really matters.

Many people have put projects and activities on hold. People think that it is enough simply to reschedule commitments. Those who are just postponing appointments, as if everything were going to go back to normal, are living in the past. The future is here and now, and there may not be a next year. There is no escape, not even for those people driving imported cars to send their employees back to work, as if they were slaves. With or without a Land Rover, if the virus catches up with them, they may die, just like the rest of us. Cities are power drainers: if the supply of electricity runs out, people will die locked in their apartments, unable to take the elevator. We didn't have the good judgment to think about the consequences of a health crisis in large urban centers, and I must confess that I feel sorry for those who live in these metropolises. Many people live alone in these city centers. We stop being social because we are living in a place with 2 million people.

In an article I read about the pandemic, the Italian sociologist Domenico De Masi quotes Albert Camus' prophetic work *The Plague*: "[P]lague can come and go without changing anything in men's hearts." De Masi mentions an excerpt from the novel that states that:

> [T]he plague bacillus never dies or disappears for good; that it can lie dormant for years and years in furniture and linen chests; that it bides its time in bedrooms, cellars, trunks, and bookshelves; and that perhaps the day would come when, for the bane and the enlightening of men, it would rouse up its rats again and send them forth to die in a happy city.[2]

I hope things don't go back to normal, because if they do, it will mean that the deaths of thousands of people around the world were in vain. After all this, people will never again want to compete for oxygen

---

[2] *Translators' note*: We quote here from p. 308 of Stuart Gilbert's translation of *The Plague*.

with dozens of colleagues in a small workspace. The changes are already in the making. It makes no sense that in order to work, a woman has to leave her children with someone else. We can't go back to that rapid pace of life, turn the ignition on in all those cars, rev up all those machines at the same time.

It would be tantamount to being a denialist, accepting that the Earth is flat and that we ought to go on devouring it and each other. Then, we will indeed have proven that humanity is a lie.

Life is Not Useful

At the moment, we are being challenged by a sort of erosion of life. As modernity, science, and constant new technological updates affect certain beings, these beings are also consumed by them. This idea occurs to me with every step we take toward technological progress: we are devouring something everywhere we go. It's becoming impossible to orient ourselves toward treading lightly on the Earth so that, shortly after we pass, it is no longer possible to trace our footprints: our marks are getting deeper and deeper. And every move one of us makes, we all make. Gone is the idea that each one of us leaves their individual footprint on the world. When I step on the ground, what remains aren't my tracks, but ours. They're the tracks of a trampling, disoriented humanity. A little baby on his mother's lap swings his little leg and sinks into the ground. Because in order to move through the world we live in today, this baby is going to use cleaning products, diapers, fabrics, materials that are eating some part of the Earth. Involuntarily, he is already preying on the planet.

I got a wonderful little plant that produces little leaves you can pick, wash, and put oil or lemon on and eat. It's full of protein. It's called a drumstick tree (*Moringa oleifera*). So it was growing in the backyard, and one day, in the middle of the afternoon, the ants found it. When I looked, there weren't any more leaves: they had eaten them all, and only the stem was left. I got annoyed with those ants ... but actually, we are doing the same thing with the planet, eating it up from dawn to dusk. Ecology was born out of a concern with the fact that what we seek in nature is finite, but our desire is infinite; and if our desire has no limit, then we are going to eat this entire planet.

Initiatives that seek to slow down our use of natural resources could suggest the notion of postponing the end of this world, but in some places that end has already arrived – whether yesterday, early this morning, or the day after tomorrow. Someone might say, "Oh, but this is so apocalyptic. He's scaring us!" But in fact, this is old news. Even in white religions, there is a story that in the beginning, this humanity spread across the planet like a plague. Their God got very angry, for they were making the world very dirty, and he destroyed it with a flood. Then he created another, brand-new world, but his humanity acted in the same chaotic and predatory way again. In other words, in white people's cosmovisions, there has also been an end of the world. They find it awkward when we talk about it because they've forgotten.

We ourselves have been causing the worlds that our ancestors cultivated to slowly disappear, without all the apparatuses that we now consider indispensable. The communities who live inside the forest feel it on their skin: they see the forest, the bee, the hummingbird, the ants, the flora disappearing; they see the life-cycle of the trees change. When someone goes hunting, they have to walk for days to find a species that used to live in that area around the village, sharing that place with humans. The world around them is fading. Those who live in the city do not experience this with the same intensity because everything appears to automatically exist: you reach out and you have a bakery, a pharmacy, a supermarket, a hospital.

In the forest, forms of life are irreplaceable; life flows, and you, in the flux, feel its pressure. What people call "nature" should be the interaction between our bodies and our surroundings – in which we know where what we eat comes from, where the air we exhale goes. Beyond the idea that "I am nature," the awareness of being alive should affect us so that we are able to feel that the river, the forest, the wind, and the clouds are our mirrors in life. I find great joy in experiencing this feeling and I keep attempting to express it, but I also respect the fact that each of us moves through the world in a different way.

In different cultures over thousands of years, we've been led to imagine that humans could act on the planet without any consequences and we've been reducing this wonderful organism to a sphere made up of elements that constitute what we call "nature" – this abstraction. We construct justifications to impose on the world as if it were malleable material: we can make it square or flat, we can stretch it, pull it. This idea also drives scientific research, engineering, architecture, and technology. Western ways of life have shaped the world as a commodity and reproduce it in such a naturalized fashion that a child who grows up with this logic lives as if it were totalizing. The information that such a child learns about how to be a person and act in society already follows a predefined script: that child will be an engineer, an architect, a doctor, a subject able to operate in the world, to make war; everything is already set. I have no interest in this sad, predetermined world. For me, it could have ended long ago. I don't bother postponing its end.

I think it's bullshit that schools continue to teach students how to reproduce this unequal and unjust system. What they call education is, in fact, an offense against freedom of thought. It's taking people who have just arrived in this world, brainwashing them, and unleashing them to destroy the world. For me, this is not education, but a factory of insanity that people insist on upholding. Maybe this pause because of the pandemic will make a lot of people rethink why they send their children to a stronghold called "school" and what happens to them there. Parents have renounced a right that should be inalienable: to pass on what they've learned, their memories, so that the next generation can exist in the world with some heritage, with some sense of ancestry. Today, anyone who talks about ancestry is a mystic, a shaman, a *mãe de santo*,[1] because "good people"[2] come out of an MBA somewhere and aren't going to keep talking about this kind of thing. They are like cyborgs who are walking around, even running large academic groups, universities, and all this superstructure that the West has built to keep everyone at bay.

---

[1] *Translators' note*: A "mãe-de-santo" is a priestess of the *Umbanda* and *Candomblé* Afro-Brazilian religions.

[2] *Translators' note*: In Brazilian Portuguese, "Pessoa de bem" or "gente de bem" often refers to conservative Bolsonaristas/ right-wing neopentescostal evangelicals. They tend to have an elite/middle-class traditional family-centered mindset, and, above all, the phrasing suggests that they are hypocrites.

The other day I made a public statement about how the idea of sustainability was personal vanity, and this irritated a lot of people. They said I was making a statement that disrupted a series of initiatives aimed at educating people about overspending on everything. I agree that we need to educate ourselves about this, but it's not by inventing the sustainability myth that we're going to move forward. We'll just fool ourselves again, like when we invented religions. There are people who feel very comfortable contorting themselves in yoga, trudging across the Camino de Santiago, or roaming around in the Himalayas, thinking they are enlightening themselves. In truth, this is just scratching the surface of the landscape. It doesn't get anyone out of a dead end.

What I am challenging here is selfishness: I'm not going to save myself from anything alone; we're all in trouble. And when I realize I won't make a difference alone, I open myself up to other perspectives. When we are affected by others, another understanding of life on Earth can emerge. If you still live in a culture that hasn't lost its memory of being part of nature, then you're the heir to it, you don't have to rescue it; but if you've gone through this intense urban experience of becoming a consumer of the planet, backtracking will be much more difficult. This is why I think it would be irresponsible to keep telling people that if we save water, or just buy organic and ride our bikes, we're going to slow down the speed at which we're consuming the world – that's a well-packaged lie.

The very idea of certification, of tests that are carried out with the materials we consume – from the packaging to the content – should be questioned before we open our mouths to say that there's something sustainable in this world of commodities and consumption. We're turning the oceans into untreatable garbage dumps, but you'll of course hear a biochemist or a smart-ass engineer say they have a start-up that's going to throw something in the water, melt plastic, and fix everything. This roguish trick even influences the choices of young people who move abroad to study in universities in Germany, England, or anywhere else, and come back to Brazil even more convinced of that mistake. So they come back brimming with competence to persuade others that consuming the world is a great idea.

While the material foundations of our daily lives are operative and functioning, we do not ask ourselves where what we consume comes from. Most of the time, people are so busy they barely even breathe or are scarcely aware of what they put in their mouths to eat. Only when there is a disaster do individuals, unplugged from their sources of supply, begin to suffer and question themselves. Those who survive a major catastrophe tend to think about changing their lives because they have had a brief experience of what it means to be alive. There are many communities living under the circumstances of loss, of catastrophe, of war. Hearing about how these people take measures to rise out of profound trauma, look around them, and start their journey over in what we call "moving on" can be instructive, but it does not replace the experience.

For two years, I have been living on the left bank of a river with the other families from among my people who, from a practical point of view, should have been removed from here, as happened with the people of Brumadinho, from Bento Rodrigues, and other places. The Krenaks did not accept displacement. We wanted to stay where the calamity had taken place. "Oh, but you don't have water!" So what? "Oh, but there's no food!" So what? "Ah, but you could die there!" So what? We know this place has been deeply affected, that it's become an abyss, but we're in it and we won't leave. It's disturbing, but it's also necessary to be in this condition in order to respond with full awareness. Awareness of the body, the mind, awareness of being what you are and choosing to go beyond the experience of survival.

Rescue missions aim to save a body that is in the midst of calamities and bring it to another place, where it will be restored. Who knows, after rehabilitation, one may even go on to function in life. This notion comes from the idea that life is useful, but life is not useful at all. Life is so wonderful that our minds try to put it to use, but that's bullshit. Life is joy, it's a dance, only it's a cosmic dance, and people want to reduce it to ridiculous, utilitarian choreography. A biography: someone was born, did this, did that, grew up, founded a city, invented Fordism, started a revolution, made a rocket, went into space; this is all a ridiculous little story. Why do we insist on turning life into something useful? We must have the courage to be radically alive, not keep bargaining for survival. If we keep consuming the planet, we won't last for more than one day.

Whether speaking to people in my village or elsewhere, I have insisted that survival is already a negotiation of life, which is a wonderful gift and cannot be minimized. In relation to life, we are like little fish in an immense ocean, in wonderful enjoyment. It will never occur to a little fish that the ocean has to be useful. It knows that the ocean is life. But we are always compelled to do useful things. That's why a lot of people die early; they give up on all this nonsense and pass on. I was once asked: "Why are so many young Indigenous people committing suicide?" Because they are finding life so stupid and this experience here so unhealthy that they prefer to go elsewhere. I know that talking about this is painful. Many families have lost kids, but we don't need to be afraid of anything, not even that.

The experience of truly enjoying life should be the wonder of existence. Someone might say: "But there are so many people who experience material challenges, who have to live in miserable, violent places ..." Nevertheless, we ourselves have created miserable, violent places, which wouldn't exist by themselves. We caused all the wars going on out there. We can't keep nurturing this idea of destiny either – when people say, "Oh, so many people suffered or went through all that disgrace or died, but it was their destiny," this is absurd. It is not their fate or mine or anybody else's. We are here to enjoy life, and the more awareness we awaken about existing, the more intensely we'll experience it without deceiving ourselves. If you need to run to a church, an ashram, a mosque, or a *terreiro*[3] to feel at peace, pay attention, because this can be an exercise, but it may not be everything you're hoping for. Religion, politics, ideologies, lend themselves to framing a useful life very well. But anyone interested in a utilitarian existence must think this world is great: an astonishing mall. The most remarkable contemporary temples are malls (including some that really are temples).

[3] *Translators' note*: A *terreiro* is a *Candomblé* or *Umbanda* place of worship.

Indigenous peoples are still present in this world not because they were excluded, but because they escaped. It's good to remember that. In several regions on the planet, they resisted with all their strength and courage so they wouldn't be completely engulfed by this utilitarian world. Indigenous peoples resist this assault of white people because they know white people are wrong, and most of the time, Indigenous peoples are treated like they're crazy. Escaping capture, experiencing an existence that has not surrendered to a utilitarian lifestyle, creates a place of inner silence. In regions that have suffered from a severe utilitarian interference with life, this experience of silence has been undermined.

In the invasion of Tibet, for example, an Indigenous group that had been living in a state of attention that cultivated inner silence and enabled the enjoyment of life for generations suffered a collision. They were thrown into the middle of this mess of the world, where silence is constantly being robbed by emergencies that seem to be happening around us. Seem to. These events have the same consistency as the footprints we are impressing on the Earth. White people's empty thinking cannot coexist with the idea of living aimlessly in the world; they think work is the reason for our existence. They have enslaved others to the extent that they now have to enslave themselves. They cannot stop and experience life as a gift and the world as a wonderful place. The potential world that we could share doesn't have to be hell. It could be good. White people are horrified by this, and say that we are lazy, that we didn't want to be civilized. As if "being a civilization" were a destiny. This is their religion: the civilizing religion. They change their repertoire, but they do the same dance, and the choreography is the same: a trampling step on the ground. Our steps tread lightly, very lightly.

I've always looked at the world's large cities as an implant on the Earth's body. As if, not satisfied with her beauty, we could make her different from what she is. We should reduce the assault on her body and respect her integrity. When Indigenous folks say: "The Earth is our mother," others say, "They are so poetic, what a beautiful image!" This is not poetry. This is our life. We are bonded to the Earth's body. When someone pierces, scratches, or harms her, it disrupts our world.

Every individual from that civilization who came to plunder the Indigenous world is an active agent of this predation. And they believe they're doing the right thing. Perhaps what bothers white people a lot is the fact that Indigenous people do not accept private property as foundational. It's an epistemological principle. In ancient times, white people lived with us, but left. They forgot who they were and went to live another way. They clung to their inventions, tools, science, and technology, were led astray, and set off to prey on the planet. So when we meet again, there's a kind of rage that we stayed true to a path here on Earth that they couldn't sustain.

It turns out that nobody is immune to the effects of climate change. The world is slowly, even if belatedly, awakening to the fact that Indigenous peoples, who are also under threat, have valuable life experiences to share. What remains for us is to live the experiences: the disasters and the silences. Sometimes we even want to experience silence, but not disaster, because it is very painful. We, the Krenak, have decided that we are inside the disaster. No one needs to come and get us out of here. We are going to cross the wasteland, we have to cross it. Or do you run away every time you see a wasteland? When a wasteland appears, cross it.

References

Books and articles

Camus, Albert. *The Plague*. Trans. Stuart Gilbert. New York: Vintage, 1948/1991.

De Masi, Domenico. "Coronavírus anuncia revolução no modo de vida que conhecemos." Trans. Francesca Cricelli. *Folha de S. Paulo*, March 22, 2020. Available at: https://www1.folha.uol.com.br/ilustrissima/2020/03/coronavirus-anuncia-revolucao-no-modo-de-vida-que-conhecemos.shtml.

Foucault, Michel. *Discipline and Punish: The Birth of the Prison*. Trans. Alan Sheridan. London: Penguin, 1977.

Kopenawa, Davi and Bruce Albert. *The Falling Sky: Words of a Yanomami Shaman*. Trans. Nicholas Elliott and Alison Dundy. Cambridge,

MA: The Belknap Press of Harvard University Press, 2013.

Ribeiro, Sidarta. *O oráculo da noite: A história e a ciência do sonho*. São Paulo: Companhia das Letras, 2019.

Rolnik, Suely. *Spheres of Insurrection: Notes on Decolonizing the Unconscious*. Trans. Sergio Delgado Moya. Cambridge: Polity, 2023.

Wallace-Wells, David. *The Uninhabitable Earth: A Story of the Future*. London: Allen Lane, 2019.

Poems and songs

Drummond de Andrade, Carlos. "Cota zero." In *Alguma poesia*. São Paulo: Companhia das Letras, 2013, p. 60.

Drummond de Andrade, Carlos. "O homem; as viagens." In *As impurezas do branco*. Companhia das Letras: São Paulo, 2012, pp. 27–9.

Gil, Gilberto. "Refazenda." In *Refazenda*. Philips, 1975.

Veloso, Caetano. "Um índio." In *Bicho*. Philips, 1977.

Film and video

2001: A Space Odyssey. Director: Stanley Kubrick. Screenplay: Stanley Kubrick and Arthur C. Clarke. Los Angeles: MGM, 1968. 149 min.

"Vernon Foster – Sobre a Pandemia/About the Pandemic." Available at: https://www.youtube .com/watch?v=R6XbXM_Gn_E.